Coffee
at Hilde's

Coffee at Hilde's

Four Provincetown Poets

Lorraine Kujawa

Lorraine Kujawa,
Hilde Oleson,
Pat Lombardi,
Margaret Phillips

iUniverse LLC
Bloomington

Coffee at Hilde's
Four Provincetown Poets

Copyright © 2013 by Lorraine Kujawa, Hilde Oleson, Pat Lombardi, Margaret Phillips.

All rights reserved. No part of this book may be used or reproduced by any means, graphic, electronic, or mechanical, including photocopying, recording, taping or by any information storage retrieval system without the written permission of the publisher except in the case of brief quotations embodied in critical articles and reviews.

iUniverse books may be ordered through booksellers or by contacting:

iUniverse LLC
1663 Liberty Drive
Bloomington, IN 47403
www.iuniverse.com
1-800-Authors (1-800-288-4677)

Because of the dynamic nature of the Internet, any web addresses or links contained in this book may have changed since publication and may no longer be valid. The views expressed in this work are solely those of the author and do not necessarily reflect the views of the publisher, and the publisher hereby disclaims any responsibility for them.

Any people depicted in stock imagery provided by Thinkstock are models, and such images are being used for illustrative purposes only.
Certain stock imagery © Thinkstock.

ISBN: 978-1-4759-9261-8 (sc)
ISBN: 978-1-4759-9263-2 (hc)
ISBN: 978-1-4759-9262-5 (ebk)

Library of Congress Control Number: 2013912037

Printed in the United States of America

iUniverse rev. date: 07/24/2013

Acknowledgments

We wish to thank Elaine Anderson, Marie Pittman, and Christie Andreson for their generosity and help. We also want to express our gratitude to Provincetown for being our muse.

Table of Contents

Part 1: Hilde Oleson 1

Lonely Street 3
Comfort Me 4
Workplace 5
Will You Dance with Me? 6
Two-Minute Flame 7
Poor Love 8
Christmas Is Memory 9
Sand 10
Question 11
Will You Play? 12
Sunset 13
Poet 14
Kurt Kurt 15
Lesson One, Please 16
Invasion 17
Debris 18
Deep Freeze 19
Almost Midnight 20
A Second Puberty 21
Two Points of View 22
Walking on Stilts 23
Teacher 24
The Company of Gulls 25
Elegy 27
Exile 28
Chorale 30
Life like an Orchid 31
Surfboard of Love 32
Travel 33
Grown Up 34
Monster 35

Part 2: Lorraine Kujawa 37

I Take My Boat 39
Whales 40
Place (Provincetown) 41
Little Blues 43
Flight 45
Autumn 46
Winter 47
Picking Tomatoes 48
Hope 49
There Was a Time 50
The Gift 51
Chance 52
My Name Is Lidia 53
I Almost Missed 54
Who Will Soothe My Heart? 55
The Fifth Date—I Drove 56
Wild Things 57
Last First Date 58
I Cannot Love Thee, Irene 59
I Was Young 60
Lines 61
The Bird I Did Not See 63
Adieu 64
Clipping Iris 65
Lament for the Stray 66
Science Project 67
Oliver 68
Classical 69
Reading Class 70

Part 3: Pat Lombardi 71

Mud 73
Hooded Merganser Comes to Duck Pond 75
Spring Pond 76
Outcrop 78
Sweet Journey 79
Brother Snake 80
Origin 81
Summer Tides 82
Questions 83
Sea Duck and Sea 84
Leaving 86
Nearly November 87
Winter Wishes 88
Lady Day's Duet 89
White Pine in Winter 90
Trinity 91
Provincetown Harbor, Winter Solstice 92

Part 4: Margaret Phillips 93

For My Grandmother, Estella Kenworthy, 1900-1984 .. 95
Leaf Stems 96
Barnyard Water Trough 97
Poem in the Shape of Walking Downhill 98
I Like the Whispery 99
My Grandmother was a Quiet Woman 100
In the Dining Room, 8:30 p.m. 102
My Grandfather Says 103
I Was Eight 104
Spring Comes 105
Shellbark Hickory 106
The Carpet 107
A Moo 108
Dusk in the Kitchen 109
Indiana, October 110
Cellar Shelves 111
The Round Woodstove 112
Phlox 113
Rich Black Soil 114
Psalm 115
When You Think 116
Orchard 118
Queen Anne's Lace 119
Homesick in Japan 120
Rules of the Roads 121
My Indiana Kin 123
I Am Sixty-Six 125
Four Cows 126
May 127

Preface

We are a little group of four
Lost in words and phrases,
Loving the sounds of our words,
Elated when the others hear unplayed melodies.
Alone, the words float in the ether.
When we put them together and they match,
A kind of elation reaches us, and we are then inspired
To write more words.
Sometimes the music soars;
Sometimes the page before us beckons.
And, oh, the days when it pours out—
More stimulating than caffeine,
More inspiring than the sunset.
The magic of the written word
Draws us together—
We know what we are all about
And what we need to do.

Hilde Oleson

Part I

Hilde Oleson

Born in the mountains, I found a new life by the sea in
 my eighties:

New friends, new impetus, new words.
After a year of sharing Wednesday mornings together,
We are ready to include you in our process of looking at
 life and putting it into words.

Lonely Street

Mass Ave stretches through the best and worst
Of Boston.
My mother died, severing that awful cord at last.
I stood on the corner, people rushing by,
Jostling, elbowing without notice,
No morning smile, no pretense of caring.
A woman dressed for power carries an open cup of
    coffee,
Steps down to cross the street
Just as a teenage hoodlum rushes by.
His backpack bumps against her as he leaves,
Coffee turning her blue dress brown.
From her lacquered lips fly torrents of abuse,
She spins on her heels, turns back to go the way she
    came.
That's what I want:
To just go back.

Comfort Me

Comfort me, O Ocean.
When my lover's eyes turn cold,
When his smile no longer warms me,
Comfort me.
Let your waves lap upon the waiting shore,
Consistent, Cconstant,
Something to count upon—
The knowledge that if I turn away,
When I come back, you will be there,
Strong and resilient as before,
Your music steady as the beat within my wounded heart,
The rhythm telling truth
My mind can hardly bear.

Workplace

Perhaps it is just a barn now,
Unused, the door for loading hay hanging
Loose, banging in the wind.
But once it was a shrine.
I wandered in, eyes dim with tears
To stand at the workbench
Where tools still held their shape,
Stayed in their orderly spots ready to be used,
Waiting to create.
The man who made his living using words,
Trying to pass the gifts he felt the Lord had given him
To mortals not so closely touched by God—
That man, known to his congregations
As a messenger from God,
Came here to bare his soul.
He spent his time commanding these tools
That never gave him "back talk" as I was prone to do.
Making gifts, useful furniture,
Structures that would outlast him;
Making sure each piece was finely honed,
Built to the perfect structure,
Meeting all his qualifications as I had never done.
A workman's glove lay inert on the bench.
I picked it up and slipped it on my hand.
Feeling the warmth still lingering there,
"Oh, Dad," I cried, "I miss you so."

Will You Dance with Me?

Mama, I stood in front of a man
I'd never seen before
And swore to him
That I would love my Joe forever
Until death parted us.
Oh, Mama, I do not want that death to come.
Remember how I used to dance
On the grass under the elm tree
When I first knew Joe wanted to marry me?
You laughed and came outside and danced with me.

But Joe led me to a new life
Where the desert stars are so bright in the dark night,
The promises so brilliant.
My eyes were filled with hope.
Now Joe spends every day practicing for war,
Learning to protect us as Marines must do.
When I open up the morning's door,
I see only cactus and tumbleweed
In a military town where there are
Twenty-nine palm trees growing in the sand
While fear grows in my heart.
In six weeks Joe will be a soldier
In a different desert,
And I will have come home to you.
Mama, will you dance with me?

Two-Minute Flame

The old couple goes so slowly down the street
Holding hands.
How sweet I think—
A love that lasts through daily grinds, distresses, joys,
 and problems.
Walking just across the road, two younger people come.
Engrossed in themselves, they do not notice us.
They are so entwined they can hardly walk at all,
Stopping to fully twist their arms and lock their mouths.
I worry that the sidewalk will melt
Beneath that holy blaze.
I see the flash of a two-minute flame,
And I remember.
This ancient heart recalls the fullest memory of life.
More vital, more sustaining
Than all the years you labored and came home
Paycheck in hand to tuck the children in,
Those fade behind the remembrance of the early days
When we too burned with a two-minute flame.

Poor Love

How sad you were
When we left you
Shivering on the doorstep.
I thought that we could pick you up again
Whenever we felt the need.
I never knew how merciless the wind
Of carelessness would blow,
How defenseless you would be.
It's been a shock to me
To hear that you are dead.

Christmas Is Memory

I touch the past.
I see the faces as I bring each treasure
Out to tie it on the tree.
This was my Mother's;
My Dad made that.
Remember when you brought this home from
    kindergarten?
That blue bulb—once I had
A whole tree done in blue.
We got this angel at the UN
When all of us were young.
The white ones were crocheted by a friend.
My sister created this—
Now she would call it "poorly done,"
As her skills have increased,
But still I love it.
The woven ones from islands far,
Made by strange hands, are so familiar now.
A duck, a swan, a dragon all reduced to trifles
To trip me up in memories
Of feeding ducks on a quiet pond,
Of the dragon that lived under your bed,
Of the Queen's swans under London Bridge.
Lost in the past,
It takes so long to fill a tree.

Sand

I saw a speck upon the sand today—
Colorless, sparkling, diving in and out
Among the other sands.
It hid a moment, then dashed back;
First hiding shyly, then displaying.
It made me think of you:
How slowly I had let your ashes dribble from my
    fingertips,
How softly they slid in to mingle with the other particles,
How separate they stayed,
How once lost they could never be retrieved.
Each moment of our lives, separate and mingled,
Each apart but joined,
Once lost could never be rejoined.
But hidden in the sands of time,
Washed ever by the waves of memory,
Kept glowing by the memory of love
Upon the shore of life.

Question

World, will you miss me when I'm gone?
Will someone else sit on this porch
To watch the glorious gold of finches hover near?
I hope that they appreciate the patterns in the leaves.
There is that lacy woven part up high,
Just a bit down the interweave of branches,
Making it dark as it reaches soft arms
To mingle with the richest firs of pines.
And where a fallen log has left a space,
The sun leaps in and sets the birch aglow.
Will someone notice how the moss
Is slowly covering up that rock?
Or how the rain is drilling out a hole
To make a drinking cup for birds?
Will they see how the fern is covering up the stump?
Or notice that the gentlest wind lets newborn leaves
Wave sweetly to the mother trees?
While guardian oaks stand tall protecting,
I notice how they bend and curve,
Adjusting to the winds of time as we have learned to do.
When sun shines into their cathedral hall,
There is no beginning and no end.
But high above a circle forms from broken branches.
Part of my soul wants to climb there to hold those
    branches,
But the other part desires to stay
Where earth is warm and I am firmly grounded.

Will You Play?

What should I do today? In this retired old age, how shall
　　I pass the day?
What can I do now that
My strength has fled, ambition gone?
I cannot clean,
No motivation and no strength.
I cannot read,
Eyes too tired from two books
Gone through in two days.
TV is worthless, no one around.
Yeah, I can play a game
On faithful friend computer.
I can pretend that it is you.
Shall I conquer you?
Give me the satisfaction of besting you at least in this,
Or shall I play to win and beat you
Viciously until you cry uncle,
Or shall I do as I have done in life?
Make little mistakes
That compound into disasters and let you walk away
Victorious.

Sunset

How quietly our little lives slip past,
One hand clasp at a time.
The smile that lit the morning leaves by noon.
Another day ends with a yawn.
To begin again with a glancing blow from a sun
That disappears behind a cloud.
The love that seemed a miracle at birth
Becomes a burden holding on
To memories that twinge and pain.
The sun sinks softly into the sea
With a gasp of color lighting the whole sky
For just a moment.

Poet

I sat with a poet last night.
Me, an ordinary human,
Sat with one of the anointed,
Sat with a man gifted by powers unknown,
Such powerful forces that they enter a human brain, give
 it impetus,
Give it words that enthrall and entice other brains.
Words that seem to come from nowhere;
Words that, standing alone, have no meaning,
But when joined by the poet in music,
Tell a story that changes our lives.
I sat with a poet making light conversation,
Foolish words to pass the time,
When he handed me a slip of paper
On which he had written that I,
Humble girl from the hills, brought up hidden in the
 mountains,
Rescued into life by the sea—
The poet said . . .
The joy that flooded through me
When the poet said
That I had joined their ranks.

Kurt Kurt

When I was young, I worked
In a nursery for blind babies.
They amazed me with what they knew
And what they could do.
One was Kurt Kurt as he called his name.
In the night he would call for me.
"Nursie, nursie," he called.
"Nursie, sing boofel morning."
I looked into the frightened sightless brown eyes
And sang, "Oh what a beautiful morning."
When it was done, he would say,
"One more time, nursie."
This time he would sing too,
And we would sing, "Ooh what a boofel morning"
Over and over
Until the terrors of the night were gone
And a little blind boy could wait
For a beautiful morning.

Lesson One, Please

Teach me life.
Teach me how to live.
Teach me how to go on
After one tragedy too many.
Teach me how to plow through the morass
Of the litter of the world,
How to walk without stepping
On the dog shit we have piled onto the silken
Sidewalks that were supposed to make us move
Swiftly into a brighter future.
Teach me how to forgive the unforgivable
And help to heal the broken hearts
That lie in heaps around me.
Show me how a life, broken, chipped, worn out
Can be of any use.
And if there is a meaning anywhere,
There must be more to life
Than only breathing.
Teach me.

Invasion

Fear invades my body like a thief.
I can feel it
Pushing hard, worming its way
Into my mind, which has put up its own barrier.
I will not quake and shiver.

Even when I feel the leech of panic gnawing,
Even when the shiver of distress sends small white
 maggots
To chew through the boundary of my will,
One small part of my mind remains guarded.
An ordinary gull soars high.
Somewhere below the boundaries of my mind,
There is a strength I have not tried.

Debris

The ocean is not beautiful today:
A gray-green color, floating debris and seaweed,
Not the strands of lace of yesterday
But mangled jams of brown and black.
A lone duck floats just out enough to avoid these tangles.
He looks perplexed—or thoughtful.
I hear him wondering,
"Where is the calm beauty that kept me floating here
    serenely?"
Oh little wild one—
I think you are the fortunate one,
Living free, no emotional engagements
To entangle you.
I see that you are wise enough to stay a bit away
Where the water is clearer
And the floating wisps cannot wind round you
To pull you into unknown territory
Like human love.

Deep Freeze

I stand in the window and weep.
Snow covers the field as far as I can see,
Nothing but white ahead with occasional searchlights
 sweeping.
Here and there are faint lines,
Tracks made by sleds or snowmobiles.
Down the pane of the window slide small frozen drops.
Perhaps it is snow or rain,
Maybe a tear.
Even the wind dare not howl.
It is silent.
The world is still.
There are no sounds allowed in my universe.
Somewhere out there,
Huddled against a fallen log,
Burrowed under a snowdrift, is the one who gave me birth,
The one who watched me every night, nourished me for
 years,
Slipped from my care this winter night.
Fate that stole her mind, somehow
Managed to move frail legs to travel through the ice
While we all slept.
The one who always buttoned up my coat, pulled my cap
 down over my ears,
Is freezing in that field.
I am the one who found the open door, the footsteps in
 the snow.
I am the one still clinging to the unworn coat, the favorite
 plaid scarf.
Blue lights tear across the sky, a siren shrieks,
But I will never thaw again.

Almost Midnight

It was the coldest night yet.
Our nostrils contracted as we breathed.
We pulled our knitted caps lower onto our foreheads
As I led two little ones through the snow
To the horse's shed.
Our feet crunched on the snow;
The moon shone on crystal-laden air
As we heard the snuffles of the old horse.
I carried the salt block, too heavy for small arms,
While they brought carrot sticks and apples instead of
    gold and myrrh.
The shed was warm and redolent as
We watched him stamp his feet and hungrily devour his gifts.
I wonder if he thought it strange
That we were visiting him in the night.
When he had eaten up his treats
And the chill was coming into our bones, we left.
"He didn't kneel," she said.
The magic tale
Of horses kneeling on Christmas Eve
Had turned out to be just that.

A Second Puberty

Entering old age is just like entering puberty.
Remember when they first began to treat you as an adult?
First talked about growing up,
Taking responsibilities?
Now it is reversed.
The same friend who would have called from her car,
"Hurry up. We're late,"
Now parks, gets out, escorts you in.
When you tip over your wineglass, no more glares and
 sighs.
"Everyone has an accident," they say.
No rushing around, take your time. No hurry.
Gone are the days of hustle-bustle.
But do I just imagine that the shopping trips are more
 infrequent?
When you protest, "No, no, I can do it," there is a certain
 amount
Of eye rolling.
When you say no, it is too difficult to go,
The topic is changed and you are excluded.
It reminds me of when we were expected to act grown up
While we still bit our fingernails and stuttered when
 embarrassed
But wanted to wear heels and learn to smoke.

Two Points of View

I woke up this morning with a headache.
I thought, "Oh Lord . . . We have guests tonight.
How will I get it all arranged?"
Then I remembered,
Thank God, the cleaning lady comes today.
What a relief.
When she came, I asked her,
"Do you ever wake up in the morning,
Already tired, achy,
Thinking, 'I wish she would clean her own damn house'?"
At first she looked shocked.
Then she smiled and said, "No, no.
I'm so glad you need me each week.
My mother is glad too,
And my sister and her three kids, all living
On an island where no one needs a cleaning lady.
There is no work there,
So my green card is a passport into life for us all.
I sing as I clean, maybe you notice.
I sing as I clean—this is for plantain, and this mopping
 buys bananas.
The toilet bowl buys a new sneaker
For the most grateful boy.
And spring cleaning?
I love it.
It buys a whole clutch of baby chicks
Who will grow to lay eggs and end as
Chicken dinners.
When you had those massive repairs,
I worked long to clean up, as it paid for my sister's
Last baby, and he is worth everything.
So I sing as I clean, and I'm happy,
So you take an aspirin and go lie down
While I make both our lives better."

Walking on Stilts

I walk on stilts through life,
Afraid to come down.
The world below is filled with fearful things.
Up here I avoid the debris of ordinary days,
Breathing the distilled air
Scented some days by the perfume of wisteria
And others by pure manure.
I know that I belong down there
Among the common souls,
But long ago someone told me
I was different,
That I should find a way to separate myself
From regular people.
They look up at me and smile.
They do not know that though I'm in full view,
I am safely hidden away
A step above, but still way down.

Teacher

You, who taught me how to laugh and love,
Have also taught me how to cry.
Is it not strange that the same hands that heal and mend
Can tear apart the very fabric that they wove?
How is it love can build a bridge between two strangers,
Weld them into an impenetrable force,
Then lower down a bomb that tears their world apart
To leave them wounded?
Yet I would not give up these years of love, the magic of
    your smile,
The courage I admired, the stubbornness that keeps you
    living,
The new life that you built for me unknowing
That the strength you gave me would be part
Of that which tore us apart.

The Company of Gulls

Low tide in autumn
Stretches on forever.

Mud flats reach toward a distant shore,
Long runs of dark sand crisscrossed by
Riverlets drizzling across deeper gullies.

It could be a lonesome time
As I sit on a stone that was submerged just hours ago,
My long skirt dragging in the mud, the dampness
Slowly creeping up my leg.

But I am not alone.
On one bright blotch of sand
There is a company of gulls.

They too sit quietly, observing.
They watch and wait as long as I.
When I stir, so do they.

One gray gull, bedraggled,
Cocks a weary eye my way.
His dullness standing out against the snow pure white of
    others.

I know how hard it is to be the one less shining,
To feel your beauty dimmed by time,
But as the quiet leads me into sadness,
He lifts his head and calls.

A noisy creaking shout
That rouses all the rest.
"Hey, world, we're here."

The entire company takes flight,
Racing, shouting, diving,
The thunder of their wings driving
All woeful thoughts away.

Hope rises with their wings.
I too arise
To go my way.

Elegy

When you don't believe it will ever be you,
It is easy to laugh at the thought
That the snowflakes that dance on the grave
Near the church
May disturb the sleep of the dead.
When you have worked every day,
Waked at the call of the alarm,
It is easy to sleep in the morning.
But as time passes by,
The body gives out its sly warning.
Sleep isn't the joy it's cracked up to be,
Eternally it may become boring,
So the call of the rain
The patter of sleet, snow falling,
May someday be a lovely distraction.

Exile

Why is it that I need
Such constant reassurance of your love?
If there is a day I do not hear your voice,

I know that doom has struck;

Your fickle heart has seen a better place
To send its warmth.

For I do not deserve
The miracle of your constancy.
The magic of your smile
Not meant for mortals like me
Who spent their childhood in exile
Cowering in the corner of the playground.
My throat felt sore
From holding in the sob that wanted to come out.
My tear-filled eye
Wanted to let loose,
But I would not,
I could not, let tears fall.
Then they would all know
That they had gotten to me.
The toss of head, the stupid grin,
The valiant haughty pose—
At such a cost would have been in vain.
They would see that I was just a kid,
Like them made of frail skin
Covering tender bones.
This time it was about the stockings.
Today I told my mother no one else would wear
Those heavy woolen stockings in a putrid shade of green.

I grimaced when she pulled them from the missionary
  box.
"They are warm," she said.
"They'll keep you warm."
Yes, as I burned with shame
Standing near the wall, pretending to be lost in thought
As kids slid by, glancing sideways at my legs,
Giggling, smiling slyly
While despondency slid over
The phony courage I had hoped to show.
Even in exile
As if it were not enough.

Chorale

Anchor me, you altos,
Keep me from soaring away
On the crystal notes of the sopranos.
I dare not close my eyes
Lest I float upward
Through the cathedral roof
To not return.
My soul has been so hungry for these sounds,
Longing to feel the touch of heaven on our earth.
One voice, one tiny thread of melody
Blending with a hundred neighbors
Melds into a richness that surrounds and heals,
That lifts us from our ordinary lives
Until for just a moment
We are divine.

Life like an Orchid

The tiny orchid blossom
Clings to life
By a tiny thread.
It was so beautiful,
Full of subtle color, fragile,
Yet strong enough to live alone for
A long time.
Now as I see only a pale remnant of that vivid past,
I realize that like my life
There will be a day
When the last petal will drop,
Leaving only the strong stem
In a beautiful handmade pot.

Surfboard of Love

I am riding the surfboard of love.
It lifts me through perilous waters.
I cling to it as we climb;
Then I rise.
Walking on water together,
Propelled by the power,
Speeding in beauty,
Breathless, racing
Into white foaming waters
Until suddenly I drop,
The surge carrying me mindless and free,
Love sliding and slipping,
Jolting away from my grasp.
But a tenuous bond holds us together,
And we rise through a tremulous sea,
Seeing new beauty, feeling new power.
Together in the vast
Unknown, we go on.

Travel

I remember those trips:
The backseat howling with children—
Sometimes laughter, sometimes tears.
"Ma, he pinched!"
"She won't move over!"
Complaints, fights, crowding,
A placid dog who felt the seat was hers,
That children would be better on the floor.
But over it all the memory that holds
Lingering after years have passed
Is the sweet calm when they fell asleep,
And I looked back to see
Sprawled on the seat in grimy disarray
The utter richness of my life.

Grown Up

How strange it is to be the mother
Of grown-up children.
The bond, the love, that cord that binds you so together
Still intact
But lives separate, distinct,
And unavailable.
I remember when I was there
For every whimper of their day,
Leaning over their cribs at night to hear them breathe.
They could not live without me then.
I was their protector, teacher, sustenance.
So somehow I thought that I was the coordinator of their
    lives,
Thrilled to watch them grow, become diverse.
Poles apart, each developed their own way,
Becoming valuable people,
Not just to me but to their surrounding worlds.
Little did I guess that the adventurous spirit I admired
Would lead them far away
Where luckily my love can reach,
But I can never stretch my arms across the continents,
So no more hugs or casual touch.
The touching of the souls enough.

Monster

You hear about him on the news
Murdering monster that he is.
You scream at him:
"How could you?" "What are you?" "You scum."
But I cry out: "No! He is my brother."
I see our mother leaning over his crib,
Her finger gently touching his round face,
Relishing the gift that love has brought her.
I recall days when he brought laughter with him
To our dinner table:
The jokes, the wit, the cynical play on words;
The cruel innuendos that kept our laughter just the least bit
Worried.
I recall that slowly laughter slid away,
But we thought adulthood
With all its challenges and problems
Had faded away the fun
That would return once he had found the way.
Oh, cruel life that pounded, beat upon that frail body
And even frailer mind,
Life's cruelties that sent more problems than one untested
    mind could bear
That took away the laughter
And leaves us with our useless love.

Part II

Lorraine Kujawa

I look for moments in nature that speak to me and look for people that weave the ins and outs of life into poetry.

I Take My Boat

When time allows,
I take my little boat
Out to sea.
Middistant between shore and horizon,
I lay my oars to rest on the side of the gunnels
And listen to the still.

As I sit atop the table of the ocean,
Far beneath me
Creatures foreign
Engage with each other,
Nose to nose.
Some jar back in mistrust
And flash swim away.
The larger ones,
Knowing their substance,
Slowly turn
And glide off in disinterest.

Some, not so fortunate,
Are gobbled up as quickly as they are seen
And live on in another.

I, above their world of swaying seaweed,
Leaning over the side of my boat,
Peering down into the water,
Have no courage to enter the deep
To take my turn in that slow blue-green dance.
I grasp my oars again
And head for home.

Whales

The whales dive deep
Leaving behind
Seagulls feeding on chum.
Having escaped death once
From baleen sieves,
The whales dive deep.
From baleen sieves
Shoot off the small fish.
Seagulls feeding on chum,
Diving for sea bread,
Cast off from gentle giants.
The whales dive deep.

Place (Provincetown)

Coffee cup in hand
I trudged between New England shelters,
Headed out to the point
They told me was "not far."
The bay to my left,
Delft Haven to my right,
Full of cottages built long
Before my birth
By strangers full of hope.
Standing strong before the wind,
That carried
The pleasure of seagulls lofting across rooftops
Headed seaward
To work the surf.

I too walk in this land of Thoreau and Eugene O'Neill.
Their lust for nature and life
Left its mark on the sands
Shifting across roadways and souls.

This is the land I saw from my sojourn with sneakers, shorts, and tee;
This is the land of salt and sea and whales and stories of heroes
Swapped across beers in darkened bars.

I reached land's end,
Rocks piled high, making a bridge across
To the lighthouse one mile to and fro.

My coffee now cooled,
I sat on the rocks looking out across the jetty.
The sea wind ran its fingers through my hair,
And I wondered
Why leave this place for the dullness of inland
Where the only waves are used-up air through wheat and
    corn.
Air that closes me in.
I am whatever befalls me here.

Little Blues

With hand extended,
My offering of chips from the bag
Enticed the gulls
In a search for food.
Frantic.

In the nearby water, rich in little Blues
And big,
Leaping to catch a glimpse of the other world
Above the line of the sea,
From a silent world
Vibrating with mystery
And hollow echoes
From far-off places.

I thought the seagulls dined there
In a split-second attack,
Dropping from the sky,
Pointed to cut into the sea
To strike a deadly blow
And carry off the meal of the day,
Tasting the soft underbelly
Served on a table of sand.

This is what I thought.
I've seen the clams as they flew with the gull and
Then were let go, execution style,
To fall on the rocks below,
Smashed shells exposing the richness inside.
This was dinner.

I wrinkled the chip bag,
And all came flying,
Young and old, white and lacewings,
Smacking the air,
Heads stretched, crying
In desperation of one who carries
Their hunger in their hearts.
A passion.

Who would have thought?
How quickly they desert the sea
For my market bag of chips.
They leave me when the bag is empty
And loft into the air,
Across the waves, heads cocked
For little Blues swimming too close to the light.

Flight

In the wind
Like knights on horseback
Seagulls aim to their destination,
Waving arms,
Banners
For the foreign nation
That owns the sea.

Autumn

The autumn shakes its leaves
From wide-armed trees,
Sweeps them in piles,
Billows up and finds a convenient corner
To swirl,
Dried and full of cluttering.
In circles,
The lucky ones,
Before the still of winter,
Dance the dance.

Winter

Sometime this winter
When weather beats
Like a drunken sailor
On a closed door,
When snow flies sideways
Biting and swallowing your breath,
Find your way to the sea.
Stand, as best you can
At water's edge
And watch waves like speeding ships
Hell-bent on cascading to the shore,
Hear the howl and rage of the wind,
And for a few brief moments,
Put your face to the onslaught
And drink it in.

Picking Tomatoes

After the rain,
We picked tomatoes
From long arms of green.

And looking for a sack
To contain our booty,
You undid your scarf,
Wrapping a circle of the silk
To make a nest,
And lay the fruit
Both red and green
Like some wild bird's eggs
With the promise of birth,
In the folds of the brightly colored patterns.

We labored
In silence,
Forgetting ourselves
Between past and future,
Like children in a field.

Hope

I've been waiting for this train,
Feet stomping in the cold.
Little hope on the long platform
Looking East
Where the train tracks merge in stillness.

I've been waiting for this train,
Hoping disappointment doesn't overcome me
Before a whistle blows
To raise my spirits
And my eagerness for joy takes hold.

I've been waiting for this train
For what seems like years
Into which promises were made,
Setting my life on hold
Until the headlights of engine number nine
Break through the dark
And tell me I was wrong.

I've been waiting for this train,
And when it gets here,
My life will begin again,
And all that I have left behind
Will pale in comparison
As it glides to a stop
On the track of this station
Where I have been waiting for the future
For a very long time.

There Was a Time

There was a time
I carved a heart on a tree in Pennsylvania
Using the knife from our picnic basket.
You, watching me in distress, whispered,
"Don't put our names in the heart!"
So fearful they would come upon us,
Finding our outcrop of love
Too foreign to accept,
And, like some Taliban sect,
Would raise up stones to put out our eyes.
Your eyes, blue and frightened,
Implored me to leave the heart
Empty.

Having no armor for your fears,
I relented.
And returning the knife to its place inside the basket,
We both leaned against the marred tree,
Shoulders touching—
The best we could do in a hostile world.
And silently we ate our tuna on rye.

On this sand spit,
Collected like smooth stones on the beach,
We children in our sixty-plus years,
Gather together, away from being strange.
And in all we can remember of the old days,
Never quite get over
The silence of an empty heart.

The Gift

I found a dead rose today,
Flattened against
The pages of a book I never read.
Its fragrance escaped
Into another time.
Somewhere between forgotten love
And passion yearning,
A hapless soul bore the gift
Now brittle beyond repair.
If only I could remember
Whose heart beat fast at my smile,
Who lingered for one last glance
As I left the room.
What sin to have forgotten
The sweet, sweet smell of love.

Chance

It took me a while
To give up on you,
Stranger.

At the party
I danced before you to catch your eye,
Laughing eyes that surveyed the room
Of dancing people in a mingle;
Never once was I separated from the drapes.

Laughing loudly I wanted my sound to catch you.
You turned,
Smiled to your friend who stood guarding your attention.

And right hand lightly brushing the air
With a dismissive wave,
You took to the door,
A vapor into the night,
Leaving the crowded room empty.

My Name Is Lidia

I am heading out tonight.
I'll let disco rule—
I'll sway with the music,
Move my shoulders with the rhythm,
Look into the eyes of good and strong women
And become who I am.
I am heading out tonight.

I'll drink wine and beer,
Toss my hair,
Show my legs.

And tomorrow at the office
When they sigh, "Poor thing, she lives alone,"
I'll smile to myself
And whisper, "My name is Lidia."

I Almost Missed

I almost missed the words
You spoke before I turned,
And in my haste I pretended
I did not hear.
We parted,
Waved and wished all well.
You went your way,
And I went mine,
And both arriving at our destinations
Thought deeply through the night
On words not spoken.

Who Will Soothe My Heart?

I planted hope
Where it would not flourish
And watered it in vain.
I held on to a wish
That was beyond common sense,
Like a child waiting for an errant parent.

Who will soothe my heart
When truth turns to face me
And the want I want
Has vanished
And my heart is still aflame?

The Fifth Date—I Drove

I knew the words
To "Our Song,"
But feared if I sang them aloud,
You'd find me rude.
Public display. No backup of personality
To cover my cretin behavior,
So I whispered as I drove;
Under my breath the notes slipped,
Hooded,
In a decibel only my ears could hear,
And when you interrupted,
Pointing out the Howard Johnson at the next exit,
I knew that when this trip was ended,
And I released you at the door,
I would sing aloud
All the way home.

Wild Things

The dog I married
Bit to my core.
My gentle nature suffered
Till the pack ran wild
And I slipped into the forest
Alone
And flew,
The sparrow that I was,
To a tall tree
Away from fear.

Last First Date

I called your home; I mailed a card;
I saw your dog out in your yard.

Somehow no one would take my bait,
Since we were on our last first date.

I brought flowers but not the bee.
I really thought the concert free.

The odor in my car will pass,
Where I had spilled some mower gas.

About your coat? I could repair,
Where you sat on my painted chair.

I was only being polite,
When your hair caught fire from candlelight.

O please forgive my pushy way,
When I dropped your house key in the bay.

I called your home; I mailed a card;
I saw your dog out in your yard.

Somehow no one would take my bait,
Since we were on our last first date.

I Cannot Love Thee, Irene

I cannot love thee, Irene.
Your lips are not for me.
The sun has set on our romance
And set it out to sea.

I cannot love thee, Irene.
You turn my head no more.
We spent the night together—
You slept, I wept, you snore.

I Was Young

We met on Sunday, early morn.
She invited me home to view some porn.
I was young and quite naïve, and
After *Sin Part II* I asked to leave.
My new amore said, "Don't be shy.
We'll soon find one to catch your eye."
We viewed part III, and I with dread
Went to the kitchen
From whence I fled.

Lines

    1.

There once was a woman I dated,
On whom all her honeys she rated.
I thought her my hero,
My rating was zero,
And now she's the girlfriend I hated.

    2.

Shelly, Shelly, softball queen,
Played real good but sure was mean.
Linda, Linda, became so smitten,
Turned that Shelly into a kitten.

    3.

Mother told me not to date
Until I was in a better state.
We kept those hearty men at bay.
I thank her still,
'Cause now I'm gay.

4.

There once was a lady with strays.
Her house filled with cats was a maze.
She cleaned and she swept
But felt quite inept.
Ten cats were in charge of her days.

5.

A-rambling I no longer go.
I found my sweetheart here.
She does the boogie to and fro
And always brings me beer.

The Bird I Did Not See

What rapture did I miss,
My head bent over book and pen?

An aha moment—
The room of faces turned toward the half door
Open to the sky and land
Where an oriole lighted
Upon a bicycle handlebar,
Bright orange and smart and
Full of life for spring,

Snapping its tail,
Looking tilt-eyed past the kitchen door
To our dull circle of faces
As we pretended to create,
Like poets do,
When all that was life
Clung tightly to the arms of the bike.

The last to raise my head,
I looked across the kitchen to the open door,
And he made a flick and disappeared,
My opportunity lost.

Adieu

I made a list
Of the flowers in my garden.
I always forget their names,
But I never forget how they wave in the breeze,
Leaning to the right and left,
Heads looking to some far-off lover
Who bids them adieu.

The dew,
Touching the heads of red and yellow and white in the
    morning,
A little kiss,
Breathed out during the night,
Remembered so long,
Till the sun slowly inhales the drops to hide
The indiscretion of the night.

Clipping Iris

I watch the peonies and flags and iris
Leaning beyond
Their walled garden plot
Into the world.
Bees hover, so familiar.

I could take scissors and clip the long stem of the iris
To take home,
Somewhere foreign
Like myself in a strange land,
To kitchen smells,
To human talk—
Away from the bees.

There is a price to be paid for resting one's weight
Too much in another world,
Giving up the past—an ache.
Bowing into the present,
Holding,
Loving them both.

Lament for the Stray

Who owns this dog,
Fur turned dry,
Untouchable odor snatching at your hand,
Head held high, running the streets
Searching, searching?

Who sent this wee lad
To run,
Apart from innocence
Chased into the cold, still yearning
For his mother's milk?

How the bleeding hearts of a civilization
Do not find this an abomination
Is in itself a scandal.

So I, the bleeding heart, stopped to buy a hot dog,
Sitting on a stranger's stoop, and
Crossed the barrier of wild and tame
And found myself a dog.

Science Project

I measure the ant.
Hard to catch, constantly moving,
I gear my tape to eye the start of him
And the end of him,
To mark the fact of him.

What skill it takes to study the who
And the what of one so foreign
To the rigors of science.

His interest in me is nil.
I am neither sweet nor useful—
Less poignant than a piece of cake.

Oliver

Fagin rose from the table,
Stout knife in hand,
Pounded its handle hard upon the breadboard:
To order! To order!
All small charges
In innocence
Looked up facing the paternal form,
Eager.
Learning from this ragged man
The essentials of life:
Be quick; be silent.
Touch nothing you cannot take.

Classical

At nine fifteen,
Martin emptied his lunch bag,
Turned it over,
And put his head inside.
The words "Hershey's Chocolate" shown
Upside down on the plastic cover.
From inside the bag
Martin pressed his eyes shut,
Inhaling the scent of fabric,
Bananas, sandwich, and apple.
He turned and waved his arms about
And walked three steps into the wall.

The class responded
With bubbles of laughter.
Martin pulled the bag up,
Light slapping newly opened eyes.
And from his stage by the pencil sharpener,
He flashed his teeth
Across the room of jubilant ten-year-olds.
Amid the floundering belly laughs
He rubbed the spot
On his head that had collided
With the wall,
And flushing brightly red,
He took his seat.

Reading Class

Light from the afternoon sun
Rested on rounded shoulders,
Student and teacher
Leaning into learning
Over the long table,
One book between two.
Tracing word by word
All that was important,
That lies at the end of fingertips
Poking out the story
That would make a long journey
Of this afternoon.

Part III

Pat Lombardi

Since I moved to Provincetown four years ago, I've spent much of my time wandering the dunes, investigating the harbor, and leaving footprints on the shoreline. I've found that the unrelenting, brutal beauty of the place has changed the way I look at the world. I have not been able to stop writing about it since I landed.

Mud

I come to the woods to walk in slop,
feel the pull
of muck and goo,
slip in slurries
of rock and rain,
think about the nature of change.

I slip backward into seepage,
learning a new
choreography:
heel, not toe, leads
down, not up—
under, not over, the surface of things.

I jump around—splash and play,
splatter filth,
wash away
sins of rigid
purity.
I love the feel,
the dirtiness—
the loss of moral heaviness.

I bend down, touch decay,
moldy solution
of scat and clay—
my response
is automatic;
it comes from ancient
parts of me
that know how reptile takes his tea.

I come to the woods to study mud
and find it has
designs on me;
it draws me down
magnetically,
releases me
reluctantly,
but not before
reminding me where I come from

and what I'll come to be.

Hooded Merganser Comes to Duck Pond

Like a monk, he wears the cowl
of his vocation and floats in silent
contemplation—past the squawking
geese and mallards, causing ripples
of sensation on our familiar pond.

Unmonklike is his flashiness:
jet-black face with golden eyes,
trapezoidal rust-red sides,
fan-shaped patch in shocking
white, and decorating chest
and back, alternating zebra stripes.

Such generous geometries:
circles, semicircles, cones,
wavy lines, and obtuse angles
combine to form a harmony—
more sculpture than anatomy.

His handsomeness is such excess
it must exist for purposes
of inspiration—perhaps
to make it clear that gods are near;
perhaps to help our worn-out senses
recognize magnificence.

Spring Pond

Ice retreats
inch by inch
from edge
to center—
leaves behind
isolated
wedge-shaped
spaces of open
water,

Elemental
murky liquid
full of silent
activity:
bubbles bubble,
send out wavelets
concentrically.

Multiple ripples'
interference
complicates
the simple pattern,
creates rhythmic
undulations—
indications of a
brewing brew.

Come early April
when frogs
and turtles
reemerge,
water lilies
undertake
aqueous migrations
to the surface

And pollen scum—
golden tracings
of wind's fury—
crowns the glory.

Outcrop

High on Nanepashemet Hill
I take my seat in a stone-cold pew
and contemplate the granite altar
rising up above my head.

My fellow congregants are these:
grass, moss, and scrub oak trees;
and lichens, most devout of all,
gather in rings of rosaries.

We bow our heads in morning mist
and listen to a chickadee
preaching the wild theology
preached to our druid ancestors:

Blessed are they who reverence stone,
who honor the virtues of the oak,
who gather in groves at solstices
and know the magic of equinox.

Wisdom is theirs who greet the moon,
who keep the seasons of the tide,
who study secrets in the stars
and salute the sun's white-fiery ride.

Sweet Journey

Who can ignore the urge to explore
the secrets of a crevice?
Certainly, the bumblebee

is drawn to irresistibly
the dimpled cleavage that divides
the lady slipper's hemispheres.

The aperture so enticing,
he buzzes in before he finds
he can't back out that bright pink door.

Forced to contort his bulging belly,
he stumbles up a narrow channel,
rubbing fuzz along the way,

and emerges from the inverted funnel
in the tiny toe at the top of the slipper,
packed with pollen, high on nectar—

as disheveled as any bee can be.
And despite confusion, despite the pain,
he's ready to take the trip again.

Brother Snake

He makes a sinusoidal sweep,
an S across
my sunny path,
then slithers off
to secret places—
but not before
he stops my heart
and stuns me with his revelations.

I marvel, retrospectively
(he's long gone now),
but still I see
the mastery
of locomotion:
limbless, wingless—
an amputee—
he curves with grace
and ease and speed
and turns his daily
constitution
into trigonometry.

How can I fail to love *his* life,
to see some of myself in him
and echoes of his life in me—
and in our fear of one another,
abiding mutuality?

Origin

There's a smell I smell
at the edge of the sea,
when humidity
and southeast breeze
mix ancient chlorine
with fishy amines,
that takes me back
to a long-ago time
before I was born
in my present form—
back to living
as a single cell
or a bobbing blob
in frothy waves—
I seem to remember
my anemone days:
two body layers,
column in shape,
when life was as simple
as passive osmosis—
one opening for food,
the same for waste
(no accounting for some
people's taste).

So don't tell me
I don't know where I come from.
Don't tell me
I don't know my place.

Summer Tides

Day Tide

Midday sun
ignites the bay.
Bright baubles bounce
from wave to wave
enticing bodies
in to play—
to feel the push
and pull of tide,
the secret joy
of buoyancy,
the lift of relative
density
lower than
the salty sea.

Night Tide

At night the moon,
the orbed maiden,
takes command,
sets a calm
reflective tone,
lays across
the darkened sea
a muted path
an undulating V
that penetrates
the heart with
tenderness
for shiny stones
and empty shells
and tiny bones
of fish.

Questions

It's always quiet
in Beech Forest
in mid-September.

Except for crow calls
not much birdsong—
even sand sleeps in the noon sun.

Everywhere signs of autumn—
mellow and mushroom
decay and rotting.

Summer's excess
turns to calmness
and a longing for the long rest.

But not quite yet
for final stasis
nothing in the woods is wasted.

Shorter days
leaves—less chlorophyll
hidden pigments come to light.

Diminishment
now prevalent
celebrates with bright.

What's left
when growth and thrust
of youth are gone—

will my true colors
make wild display
after my green mask fades away?

Sea Duck and Sea

She stands on the breakwater,
next to a gull,
keeping silent
company.
Waves caress her feet
repeatedly
and promise more;
the shy gull flies
away—she stays,
enjoys the rhythmic,
salty play.

Soon high rollers
massage her thighs;
she calls out grating
cooing cries
and keeps her eyes
on the soft horizon
as rushing tide
picks up the pace,
dampens her lower
downy places.

Then Neptune roars in,
fingers curled,
swirls an aqueous
filigree
over her fluffy
anatomy—
laps and slaps
and pats her belly.
(Now her legs
have turned to jelly.)

She stands no more
but folds her folds
into the foam,
merges with
her second home,
and rides the swells
contentedly
till I can see
no difference between
sea duck and sea.

Leaving

Some leaves drop early;
some wait
for gusts of wind
then descend
in noisy groups;
some hang on
till season's end
when breezes
bring them down
one by one.

The fall of fall
is not from grace—
orange origami
drift in air—
a weightless dance
through time and space—
as if the force
of gravity
gave way to the whims
of a northwest wind.

I hold an oak leaf
in my hand—
it looks like leather,
feels like silk,
is tough, supple,
flexible—
a minute ago
part of a tree,
now I see
up close the beauty
that remains.

Nearly November

Crisp leaves in gold
and brown persist—
dull remains
still make a claim
on life and fill
the space between
the dunes with beauty.

I sit on the roots
of a half-dead scrub pine;
take notes—try
to write my way
through shorter days,
think words will tell me
how to live in
seasons of loss.

Finally,
I put my pen down,
pay attention
to the silence—
the message is written
in the trees:
accept the darkness,
tolerate the cold,
release the need
for more.

Winter Wishes

I wish I had a
caterpillar,
a blue-and-orange caterpillar
creeping up my sleeve.

I wish I heard
starlings singing
off-key a cappella greetings
to the morning sun.

I wish I saw
leaf buds unfurling,
turning trees, and sandy hills
from gray to green.

I wish I smelled
wild aromatics
seeping up from creeks and cracks
in spongy soil.

I wish I hadn't
wasted so much
time inside in books in writing—
living in my head.

I wish I'd gone outside
instead.

Lady Day's Duet

The academic chickadee
shivers in an evergreen
outside my window;
his thin black cap
and feathered gown
are not enough to keep
him warm in damp
December weather.

He sings a lonely two-note
song that floats above
the freezing rain, slips
through double Thermopane,
and circles round my old CD—

Then lands—with audible
fee beees—in the middle
of Billie's melody:

Love is funny
or it's sad;
it's a good thing
or it's bad . . .

but beautiful.

White Pine in Winter

Separated, sheathed in ice,
each needle bundle
forms a spike—
lost is flexibility;
gained is crystalline
rigidity and a hoary
kind of strength.

But stronger still
is morning sun,
and drip by February drip,
brittleness succumbs
to tender touch.

I'll be patient—I can wait
until the warmth
has done its job. Then
I'll squeeze your
swirling boughs
and kiss your leaves again.

Trinity

Eider, gull, and baby seal
lie down on the holy float
on freezing January mornings
whenever the sun is out.

They hug the edges,
avoid the center,
eye each other with care,
and create safe space
from the sides and angles
of a seven-foot wooden square.

And they stay there all day long.

So if on a winter's day salvation
feels like the sun on your back,
then sometimes the only way to salvation
is to lay your tender tummy down
on a dung-encrusted pallet
in the middle of the sea

And offer to fellow travelers
your vulnerability.

Provincetown Harbor, Winter Solstice

In south by southwest sky, I see
red, yellow, blue, some green:
rainbow spectrum without rain
as if Newton left his magic prism
in a corner of the bay.

Soon red begins to swallow yellow;
orange tones take control—
turn puffy cumulus underbellies
by alchemy to gold.

Impatient, red blurs into blue;
purpling streaks stretch south and east,
meet with pink, swirl into gray—
surrender to the passing day.

What's left of blue seeks hottest red—
violet edges start to spread, but
violet fades, turns its back,
unwilling to acquiesce in black.

Black refuses all compromise
and fills the semicircle of the sky.

So starts the darkest, longest night.
I seem to welcome loss of light,
inward-turning hints of rest—
the solemn sense of
nothingness.

Part IV

Margaret Phillips

In the summer of 1989, I visited Plimoth Plantation in Plymouth, Massachusetts, perhaps the best known living history museum in the United States. As I moved from place to place, between houses, along fields and paths, something was powerfully familiar. It wasn't the little timber-framed houses or muskets or the log meetinghouse. Somehow it was the smooth, foot-pounded surfaces of the paths, the weeds between fields, the smell of the cows and pigs, the weather-gray boards in fences and siding. It was my grandparents' farm in northern Indiana in the 1950s, a place of many family visits and overnights during my growing-up years. This was "living history"; elements of my grandparents' way of life were things of the past. Part of me was also part of the past. These poems attempt to catch something of that time and those people, especially my grandmother.

For My Grandmother, Estella Kenworthy, 1900-1984

If I could step, just one moment,
into the next room to ask her
about the hand-cranked machine,
big as a car engine,
that sat in the storage room
of the milk house.

It's not a car engine;
it's made of wood,
and its green paint
has flaked off along the edges and sides.

It's a winnower. It separates wheat
from chaff. What does that mean?
A machine that clacks and chuffs.
Dust circles in a wave of sunlit sparks.

The bare, slanted board prevents
what? Grain or chaff from escaping?
The inside is bare wood—why? To prevent
paint chips from chipping into the grain?

Why is it so beautiful?

I long
to go back, wish to overtake . . . something,
a knowledge,
now lost,
of myself, knowledge
that I would
never die.

Leaf Stems

My question comes from
the border where the hollyhocks
edge into the yard.

I am not hollyhock
nor hollyhock blossom.
I am not mown grass
nor tall leaf stems.

The stems of the hollyhocks
are taller than my head.
I look up at the stamens
covered in yellow pollen.

I brush hollyhock pollen
across my cheeks and lips.
I belong in the border.
What am I?

There should be such a thing
as myself so I can be named
after the plant of myself.

The wind pushes
across my bare arms.

Barnyard Water Trough

On the outside where it sweats, green moss.
Inside and under water, red particles
of iron, like dust, cling to the walls. I erase
them with my hand. The sun slants
onto my arm through the cold water.

The workhorses pull long drafts
of silver into their mouths. The cows walk away
with strings of water hanging from their chins
to the ground. They'd waited their turns.
From trough to milking barn, their hooves
print the dust.

Poem in the Shape of Walking Downhill

The
  footpath
  curves
    around
      the
       house,
         bending
           downhill
             to
               the
               fields.
              It
       is
          narrow,
               smooth,
             and
               flat.

                    The
                    short
                     grass
                       falls
                     over
                    the
                    path's
                    edges
                    like
                    naturally
                    curly
                      hair.

I Like the Whispery

I like the whispery
pale tangerine clouds of morning.

I like thunderheads,
rumbling and shrugging and being grumpy.

I like soggy clouds,
dripping over eaves and tree limbs.

I like to see
dragons in clouds, toasters in clouds, earrings in clouds.

I like to get dizzy
watching clouds moving fast.

I like long, slender,
transparent blue scarf clouds in long, slender drifts.

My Grandmother was a Quiet Woman

In winter
she wore overshoes,
a wool coat, and
a wool babushka
over the two gray knobs
on the back of her head.

She thumped the chopping block
with a piece of firewood
half split and hanging on
the ax.

Spring mornings
inside the henhouse, she showed me
how to reach under the chickens
for eggs as warm as her hand.

At the dining room table
her flour-dusty hands
jabbed at flour and lard
to shape the pie dough.

She wore dentures;
when we ate,
she chewed meat
in the front of her mouth.

Sometimes I looked at her,
and she looked back at me.
Her eyes
were blue.

After supper dishes
she crocheted,
and then she got up
to put wood in the stove.

Now I am older than she
was then. I cannot go
to her house or rock
in her rocker. I look

at my hands
and see my thumbnails
like hers.

In the Dining Room, 8:30 p.m.

A little earlier
Grandmother
carried in
pieces of wood
so big she had to
pound them
into the woodstove.
The fire will burn
all night.
Now she's in a chair
pulled out from the table.
She smells of bread,
hard water, cold air.
Her white hair—
two daytime buns
behind her head—
has become
an electric shower
over her nightgown and
down her back.
Her fingers divide it
behind her head
and then braid,
walking down the hair
over her shoulder.
She's thinking of tomorrow.
Her eyes see me.
She says, "Time for bed."

My Grandfather Says

Lime puts sweetness back into the acidy, yellow urine in the gutters in the cow barn with the big black-and-white cows that watch my grandfather and want to know what he wants. He wants them peaceful in their stanchions, chewing their cuds. He wants their heavy bags of milk comforted by the way he washes their teats; he pulls each one with a washrag; the cows relax their backs like a sigh. Then relief from the milking machine. And with October cold at night, they stay in the barn where they're together and can hear each other breathing. The barn fills up with their breaths, and some lie down in the hay. I want to know if they are sad because they miss their calves. I think the cows remember their calves sucking, their bags emptied and relieved, like Cora whose long tongue licked cowlicks into her bull calf's hair around his horn buds. He butted her belly to move her so he could latch onto his favorite teat and straighten his legs under her and lift his head to look and suck, suck as if nothing would ever change.

I Was Eight

when I went into the barn
and saw the hind legs
of a calf dangling
out from under
the tail of a standing cow,
the milking parlor empty
but for my uncle
and grandfather
and this strange being

and

the cow kicked and the half calf
shuddered,
my brain asking how
the front legs and head
come out,

and

my grandfather's voice
said "We wait
and then pull. She'll be
all right,"

but

I ran
to the house
and shoved my face
into my grandmother's apron
demanding to
go back,
go back.

Spring Comes

like a cranky child
and stamps in scraps of dirty snow.

Spring comes
with a smirk
and her eyes closed.

Spring comes
with her wet kisses
and tantrums.

Shellbark Hickory

The blue shadow divides into limbs and twigs
on the snow, curves into drifts and
shallow hollows around fence posts.

In spring, the branches spread sensitive
tips into crisp snow-fed air, into the warmth
of the sun, yearn into leaf buds.

The farm's summer ditch is draped
with flowering grass and the hickory's plain
trunk holding its great green head.

The hickory nut is a sweet kernel
squeezed in a tight fist, into deep
October. Yellow leaves light the cool

evening, like candles.

The Carpet

My mother likes to go to the farm where she grew up.
She puts us and the basket of diapers and bottles
and baby clothes for my sisters into the car and drives
to the farm. I like to go there too. In winter I can
get bundled up and go out to the barn, or I can look
at books in my grandma's living room. I like to lie
on the floor there so I can smell the carpet,
which smells like a wool blanket. The closer I am
to the woodstove, the better the carpet smells.
It has a pattern of blue and red and brown flowers
over and over. My grandma's proud of the carpet,
but I like lying on the floor so I can smell the carpet
that smells like wool, like a blanket, like mittens,
like winter.

A Moo

It's true:
cows moo.
They can-
not coo.
But have
you a
clue that
cows ex-
ude ex-
pressive
moos? That
cows go
through a
"Yoo-hoo,
you loved
human"
moo? That
calves sough,
"Where's Ma-
ma" moos?
They do.

Dusk in the Kitchen

It's quiet over splash and clink,
except for our moving feet.

We are drying. We are putting away.
I'm wiping counters.

We push damp hair away from our faces.

The window that moments ago
showed us the backyard maples

casts back an empty room.

Indiana, October

In slow motion

a forest fire

yellows

the hawthorn

fiery with thorn jets.

Orange

heat

sears

this tree

red,

these trees

aflame

Cellar Shelves

Like library shelves
but with glass volumes that are mason jars of cherries
and blackberries—jars that open to episodes of pie;
sequels of peaches and applesauce;
exploits of tomatoes, beans, purple grape juice
beside the atlas of the potato bin—its filling-up thunder,
its whiff of loam a map of earth.

The Round Woodstove

My grandfather has his Civil War book;
my uncle his comics.
My grandmother ponders popcorn versus fudge.
Firelight from the round woodstove
glows like the heart of the room.

Phlox

It's warm.
In tall grass with
dried blades mixed in,
phlox blossoms stand
on stiff stems radiating
half hemispheres of blossoms,
white and not perfectly round, but
perfectly not quite round.

Rich Black Soil

Rich black soil here
enriched the old-time folk,
who, seeing the horizon
across the farm flat acres,
built gabled galleon houses
to ride their homestead rises.
They planted hardwood groves;
the soil eager to bear shade,
green, leaf sound of water
for the perishing summer,
windbreaks and drift breaks
for the slash of winter.

Psalm

Zinc washtubs—square,

gasoline washing machine bangs its one cylinder,

clothes splash in dark water,

stones in the milk-house wall painted white,

washing machine wringer squeezing little waterfalls

from overalls and blue chambray shirts.

When You Think

When you think of a pig field,
maybe with a slant-roofed shed
where the pigs sleep at night
or escape the sun on a hot day,
you think it smells. But expecting
a stink means you've never
been there. Fact: mud in a pig field
smells like wet dirt after a rain,
that's all. Pigs wallow in mud;
they don't defecate in it. For that,
they find a far corner of the field,
and all the pigs use it. Pigs
are not stupid.
Pigs don't sweat. Pigs lie down
in mud and get up muddy to let
the mud dry and cool them off.
This is pig nature.

My Uncle Jim, sixteen, and I, nine,
climb to the roof of a pig house
to read comics. But it's hot,
and Jim stands up and walks
to the top of the roof and turns
around like a platform diver;
his feet grasp the edge of the roof.
He proclaims,
"I will now leap up from this roof!
I will touch my toes in midair!
I will land on my feet!"

His arms are at his sides. He raises
his arms and jumps.

He hangs against the sky—
his fingertips nudge the toes
of his sneakers.

He brings his arms
up and pulls his legs together—
but before they get there, his butt
slams down on a huge nursing sow.
She shrieks.
His legs clench her belly.
She runs. Her teats flap.

I see his journey.
I see his fall.

In the hog wallow, a dark
figure stands up,
covered in mud
but only mud,
owing to the nature of pigs.

Orchard

Push

your damp hair back from your face. You'll cool off
  some,

but the heat will continue to rise around you.

Choose

the big, low-limbed Northern Spy

in the almost level evening sun.

Sit

near the trunk on a branch; thread yourself

between the rung-like boughs.

Think

of this spot in the purple and orange dawn,

of noon today when the mourning dove sat in a high
  forked bough.

Queen Anne's Lace

They bow
to the nobility
of nature, to the regal
sky and the emerald field.
The graceful
bowing heads of
a queen's lacework,
listening to the peaceful wind,
oblivious to their own noble beauty.
With nodding
purpose they part
for a child wading in
breast-deep to become one
of them, cleanly and calmly
and beautifully as eternal Queen Summer.

Homesick in Japan

An Indiana farm still lives in me;
I listen to the bell of temple hush
and miss my home that's far across the sea.

Japan's sun rising orange through cherry trees
ignites and raises rays of yellow dust
from a farm in Indiana still in me.

This air of summer draws me to be free.
It sharpens edge of thorn and leaf and bush.
It makes me long for home across the sea.

I see red zinnias on a windowsill
when I close my eyes to hear an Asian thrush.
An Indiana farm lives in me still.

Japan's cold breath of mountain aerie
inspires the hawk to soar on stony gust.
But blowing prairie grass is home to me.

And Midwest afternoon has roots in me;
I hear the supper voices call at dusk.
A farm in Indiana's still in me.
My home is much too far across the sea.

Rules of the Roads

Japan's
country roads adhere to the close edge of house and field,
    clench tight
to rises, hills, outcroppings. No arable square centimeter
    wasted on travel.

Japanese country roads call for mist to rise from terraced
    paddies
into morning sun. Afternoon reflections of the clear sky say

home is near, around the big rock shaped like the
    neighbor's elbow
as he minds the irrigation wheel sloshing pale water into
    the next terrace

a few steps up. Ripe rice also follows the road's rule:
heavy stalks ready
for reaping must bow respectfully, and with thanks, over
    the road.

Indiana's
country roads lie in a grid, travel north and south or east
    and west.
Of course, there are other roads, ones that curve around a
    lake

or follow along a stream to a solid bridge crossing, but
    not many.
These few exceptions make the grid rule into a good rule,

a rule that flexes and expands for beauty, that states
    country roads
be lined with milkweed and Queen Anne's lace and with
    thick oaks,

their wide leaves dark under pale dust lifted from loose
    gravel
on the road, which must lie in three long lines looking
    into the sunrise,

toward town, and into a ripe orange sunset coming back.

My Indiana Kin

Look at them look at me
around my silent grandmother.
She is dying, and they
wish she would say
a word or touch them or look
at them. They say
nothing for her to look
at them. Her face
a twist in their hearts,
the past a thing of the past,
they no longer think
about back home, about cold hard
water, their mother washing
farm dirt back to the ground.
They are painting a picture
of this old woman as she
stood on the porch,
her strong hands on her hips,
her loud voice calling
their names—Matt! Miriam!
Reba! Fred! Richard! Supper!
Wash up! Victor, bring the children!
She is dying now,
voice silenced by a stroke.
The cost of not hearing her
grates in their hearts:
where they would come home
to supper,
where they would wash up
and sit moist and combed,
waiting for Pa to spoon
out boiled potatoes,

waiting for Pa's voice silenced long ago
to say "For what we have received, bless us,
oh Lord." Oh Lord, a silent prayer
to a cold God. Their mother
will be strong as death.
Look at me look at them
around my dying grandmother.
They are wishing
for a word.

I Am Sixty-Six

I was twenty
when you were sixty-six
and still lived on the farm.
You walked
out of the kitchen
in those black shoes
with fat two-inch heels,
Buster Brown laces.
Your shoulders rocked a little.
You pecked
my cheek;
you smelled like hard water;
your ear was warm
on my ear.

When you were sixty-six,
you had crocheted for fifty years.
No hope for me to learn—
your patience worn thin
like the blade of the paring knife.
But your crocheting needle
swam and dove,
like the bow of a violin.
Your thread-guiding hand
played the bass line
as your lips tightened
and relaxed,
eyes up at me,
down at the dresser scarf
in a rubato against
the rhythm of the rocker.

Four Cows

Four cows stand in the shade

of the small catalpa by the fence.

Their slow jaws grind.

Chickens scratch in the hen yard.

Breaths of warm alfalfa.

I could scrape blue handfuls

off the sky.

May

I will walk down to the orchard.
   I will see my grandmother there.
And stand once more under the white blossoms.
   She will be wearing her apron.
To listen to the grumbling bees
   Her eyes will be on the blossoms.
And see again the petals against the sky.
   And the wind will blow her hair.

CPSIA information can be obtained
at www.ICGtesting.com
Printed in the USA
FFOW03n0442090415
12516FF